Casting all your care upon him; for he careth for you.—1 Peter 5:7, KJV

AF869918

Who Cares

Bernard & Marjorie Palmer
Illustrated by Lucille Marsh

Bethany Fellowship INC.
MINNEAPOLIS, MINNESOTA 55438

Copyright © 1979, Bethany Fellowship, Inc.
Printed in the United States of America

Who cares for the sparrow,
sassy and loud?
He's not very big,
but oh, he's so proud.
Some people don't like him,
but he doesn't care.
He acts as if
they aren't even there.
Who cares for the sparrow,
sassy and loud?
God does. That's who.

Who cares for the cuddly baby seal?
He's so tiny and helpless he can hardly squeal.
He's left all alone when his mom's at sea,
and he can't fix breakfast, or even tea.
Who cares for the cuddly baby seal?
God does. That's who.

Who cares for the lamb
that's strayed from the fold,
and keeps him warm
when the night is cold?
Who keeps him safe
from the wolf and bear,
and makes him brave
when his mom's not there?
Who cares for the lamb
that's strayed from the fold?
God does. That's who.

Who cares for the whale so big and strong?
His mouth is as wide as you are long,
or, wider by far, to speak the truth.
But he won't bite. He hasn't a tooth.
Who cares for the whale so big and strong?
God does. That's who.

Who cares for the dolphin,
who's happy and gay?
He makes you want
to jump and play.
I'll have you know,
he's an acrobat.
Now, tell me quick,
what you think of that.
Who cares for the dolphin,
who's happy and gay?
God does. That's who.

Who cares for the fawn
when he's all alone,
when he's lost in the woods
so far from home?
Who guides him back
to the mother deer,
so she can wipe away
all his tears?
Who cares for the fawn
when he's all alone?
God does. That's who.

Who cares for the mole
digging in the dirt?

He can't see where he's going,
but that doesn't hurt.
He keeps right on digging
his own little hole,
and he won't quit
'til he's finished his goal.
Who cares for the mole
digging in the dirt?
God does. That's who.

Who cares for the snail
crawling ever so slow?
He doesn't hurry;
he has too far to go.
It's good that he takes
his house with him.
It would cost too much
to stay at the inn.
Who cares for the snail
crawling ever so slow?
God does. That's who.

Who cares for the wiggly, wobbly calf?
When you first see him, you'll want to laugh.
You wouldn't think he could stand at all,
and you're mighty sure he'll never grow tall.
Who cares for the wiggly, wobbly calf?
God does. That's who.

Who cares for the snowbird in the storm?
He doesn't fly where it's nice and warm.
He likes to stay where the big drifts blow,
scratching for food in the ice and snow.
Who cares for the snowbird in the storm?
God does. That's who.

Who cares for the dolphin,
the snowbird, the seal?
Who sees that the sparrow finds a meal?
Who watches over the giant whale,
who's much too big for your sand pail?
Who cares for the dolphin,
the snowbird, the seal?
God does. That's who.

Dear Parent:

This little book can be used in several different ways as a teaching tool with your child.

Here are some suggestions:

First: Let your little listener answer the recurring questions aloud as you pause in the reading. The answer is always the same: "God does."

Second: The next time through, point out the name of God every time you come to it. The third time (or very soon thereafter) the children will be able to put their own fingers on it as you read along.

Third: Ask the children which little creatures they would like to be. They are sure to have favorites.

Fourth: Encourage them to talk about the things they especially like in the story.

Fifth: Discuss some of the instincts they have seen in animals they know, or some of the things they are glad God made, or some ways in which God has shown His love to them or has been good to them.

Sixth: After a few trips through his little WHO book, your youngster soon will be able to tell the story of each page alone. Encourage the little ones to do so.

Finally: Every time you finish going through these pages take a few moments to talk about God from your own experience. Then pray with your children briefly, thus developing a sense of the nearness, the reality, and the continued concern of God.

The Publisher